Dedicated to my mother Teresa.

That Mean Old VIRUS

Library of Congress Cataloging-in-Publication Data
ISBN: 978-0-578-92808-1
ASIN: B0578928086 (eBook)

What is a virus?

A virus is a living thing that you and I can't see.

It lies around on things we touch, eat, and sometimes breathe.

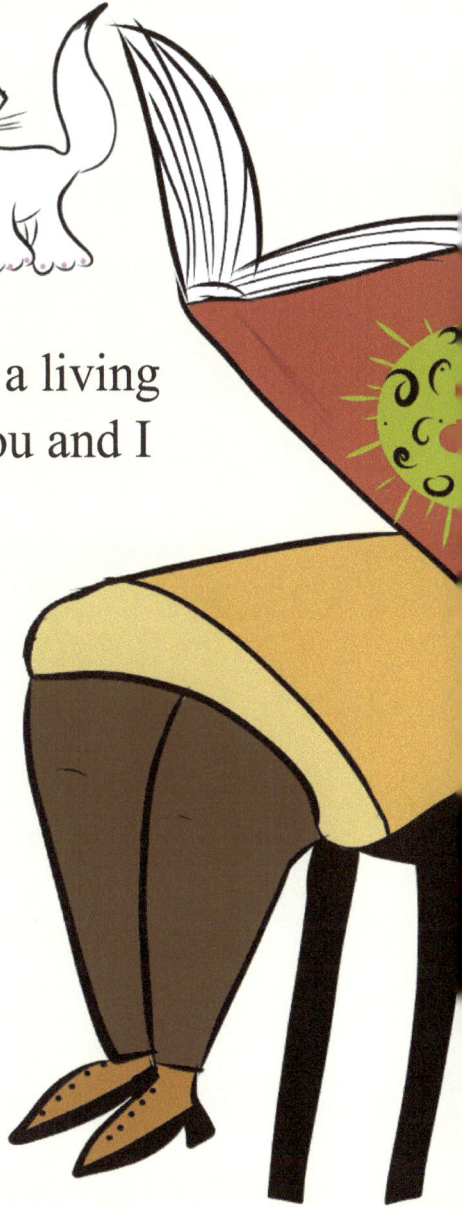

And because a virus is invisible, and no one knows it's there, that mean, old, ugly virus could be hiding *anywhere*!

Where, oh where, could that virus be, if I cannot see it hiding from me?

On the things we touch, on things we eat, and sometimes in what we breathe.

That virus could be *anywhere*, even on you and me!

Oh me! Oh my! On me, and you?

Oh me! Oh my! What should we do?

We should wash our hands, and rinse our hands, until they are clean, with warm soapy water - front, back, and in between.

And *don't* forget your thumbs, because that *mean, old, ugly* virus is one *sneaky* bug-a-bum!

And this is why we wash our hands, and thumbs so much - so much!

To keep off the germs that get on our hands, from all of the stuff we touch.

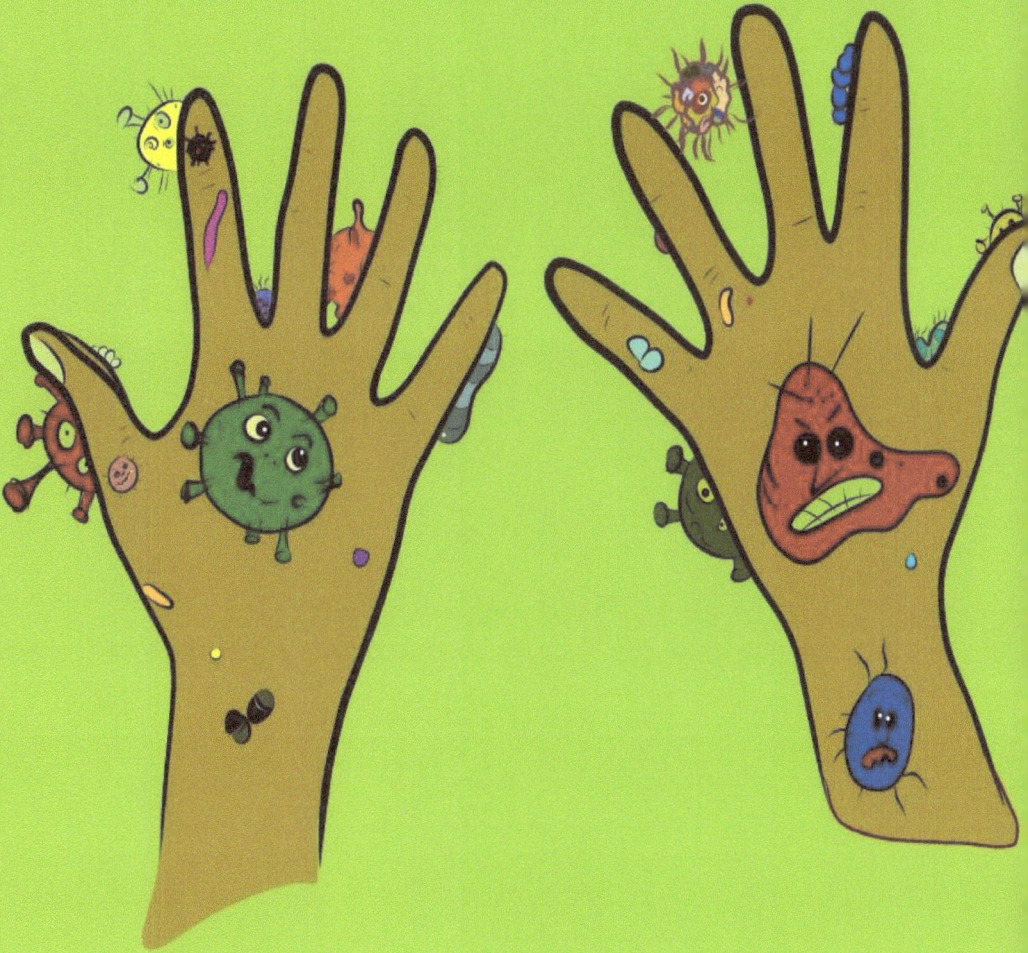

Like boxes and books, doorknobs and handles; desktops and chair backs, for example.

Paper and plastic, pencils and crayons; the monkey bars, and sliding boards, the things we play on.

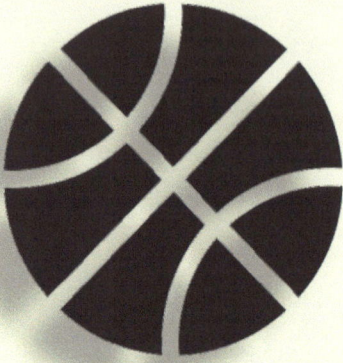

Basketballs, dolls, toy trucks, and swings, a virus could be on almost anything!

And since spreading a virus is easy to do, washing your hands is all up to you.

Scrub them 1, 2, 3, 4…, 20 seconds *long*, about the time it takes to sing the happy birthday song!

Now, let's pretend to wash our hands to see if this is true.

So, when it's time to wash *your* hands, you will know *exactly* what to do!

On the count of three let's sing-along to see if this is so.

If it is - tell a friend to teach a friend so that *everyone* will know!

So get ready to sing, and follow my lead; we will begin to sing on three.

If you are ready to sing with me –
One… Two… Three…!

Happy Birthday to YOU,
Happy Birthday to YOU,

Happy Birthday,
Happy Birthday -
Happy Birthday to YOU!

And many, many *more*!

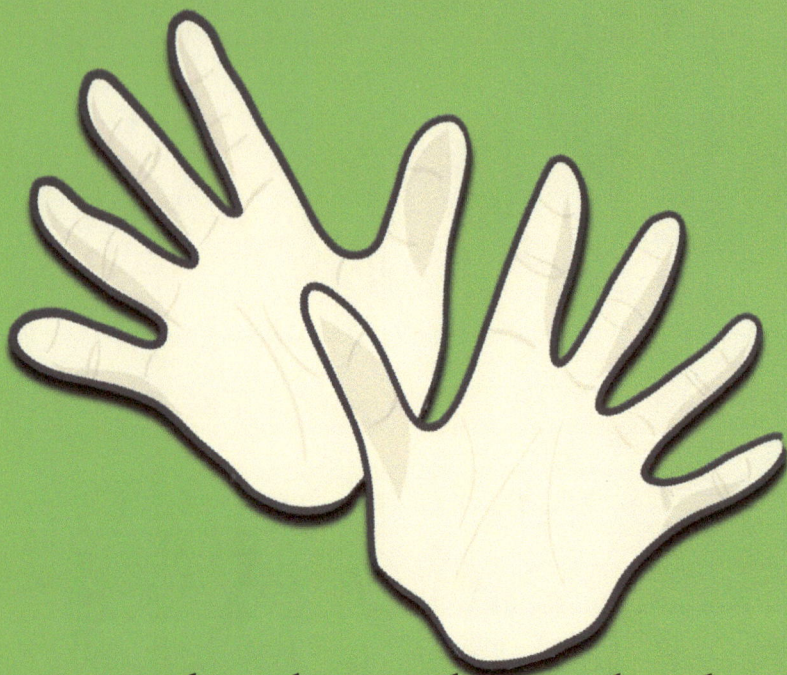

If you remembered to wash your thumbs, and in between each finger, then you are by far, the smartest kid in class, you little hum-dinger!

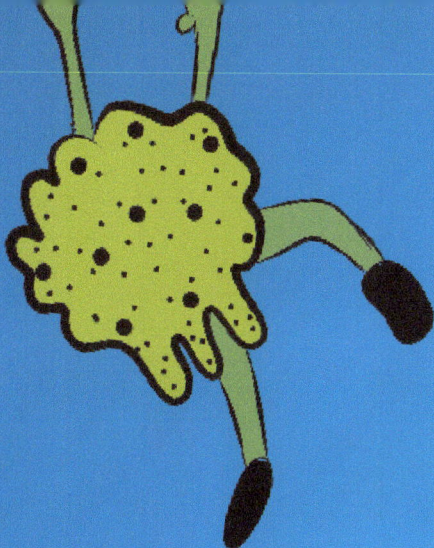

And, even though you wash your hands, you should *always* be aware, because that *mean, old,* virus could be hiding, on things we like to share.

Can *you* think of anything you have shared, will share, or share-alike, like your bus to

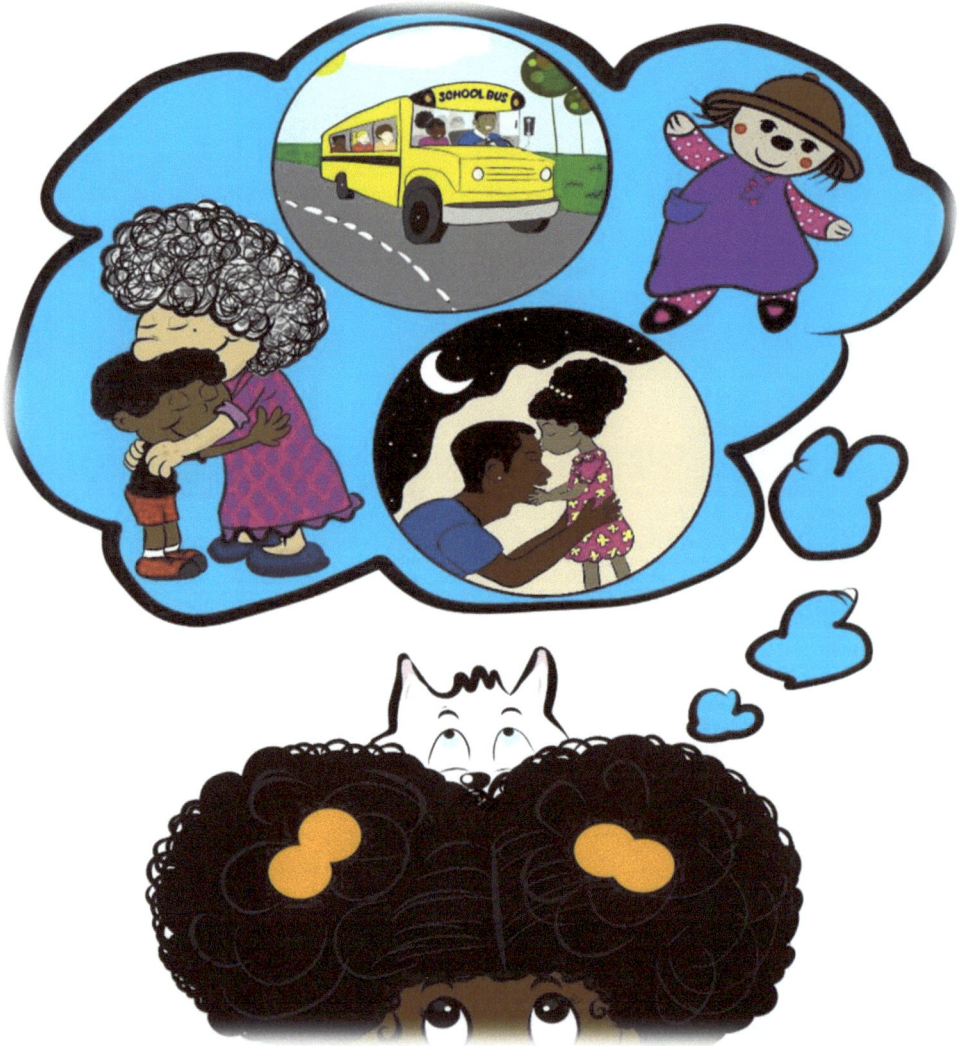

school, a Christmas toy, a hug, or a kiss goodnight?

Well, there is one *big* thing that you and I cannot see that the *whole* wide world *must* share!

We need it to breathe; we cannot live without it, and that, my friend - is the air.

But, how does a virus get in the air?

I'm sure you would like to know.

By breathing, sneezing, coughing, and wheezing, through our mouths and noses!

And, to kill a virus, or slow it down, we have to wear our masks, so that the spread of the virus, will not get inside us, and make us sick or sad.

Because once it's inside, it will multiply, by rocking, rolling, and shaking!

It will invite all its friends over to have a big party, until *you* feel sick, and are aching.

So, remember these rules, and remember your thumbs, bah-da-bing, bah-da-boom, bah-da-bum!

"Cause by doing your part, to beat that old virus, will show'em how it is done.

So, rule of thumb number one, is to wash your hands and thumbs.

Keep your hands to yourself, and away from your face, and _never_ forget rule one!

Rule of thumb number two, will protect me and you.

Stand six feet apart, while wearing our masks, is *all* we have to do!

Rule of thumb
number three, is
made for you and me.

When you cough or
sneeze, use a tissue
please, or cough and
sneeze in your sleeve!

Please, and thank you!

What To Remember:

- DO NOT touch your eyes, nose, or mouth with your hands.
- Wash your hands in warm, soapy water for (20 seconds) or use hand sanitizer.
- Stand and play 3-6 feet apart.
- Wear your mask in public places ALL the time.
- Cough and sneeze into the creases of your elbows and sleeves.

www.ingramcontent.com/pod-product-compliance
Lightning Source LLC
LaVergne TN
LVHW010024070426
835508LV00001B/43